THIS MONEY TRACKER BELONGS TO

_____

_____

_____

_____

_____

_____

				TOTAL BALANCE: _____	
DATE	NOTES	WITHDRAW	DEPOSIT	AMOUNT	TOTAL

SPECIFIC ITEMS I AM SAVING UP FOR

ITEM DESCRIPTION	COST	WHERE TO GET IT	HAVE I GOT IT YET?

WAYS TO EARN MONEY

DATE	HOW TO EARN IT?	AMOUNT	HAVE I EARNED IT?

TOTAL BALANCE: _____

DATE	NOTES	WITHDRAW	DEPOSIT	AMOUNT	TOTAL

SPECIFIC ITEMS I AM SAVING UP FOR			
ITEM DESCRIPTION	COST	WHERE TO GET IT	HAVE I GOT IT YET?

WAYS TO EARN MONEY			
DATE	HOW TO EARN IT?	AMOUNT	HAVE I EARNED IT?

			TOTAL BALANCE: _____		
DATE	NOTES	WITHDRAW	DEPOSIT	AMOUNT	TOTAL

SPECIFIC ITEMS I AM SAVING UP FOR

ITEM DESCRIPTION	COST	WHERE TO GET IT	HAVE I GOT IT YET?

WAYS TO EARN MONEY

DATE	HOW TO EARN IT?	AMOUNT	HAVE I EARNED IT?

TOTAL BALANCE: _____

DATE	NOTES	WITHDRAW	DEPOSIT	AMOUNT	TOTAL

SPECIFIC ITEMS I AM SAVING UP FOR

ITEM DESCRIPTION	COST	WHERE TO GET IT	HAVE I GOT IT YET?

WAYS TO EARN MONEY

DATE	HOW TO EARN IT?	AMOUNT	HAVE I EARNED IT?

TOTAL BALANCE: _____

DATE	NOTES	WITHDRAW	DEPOSIT	AMOUNT	TOTAL

SPECIFIC ITEMS I AM SAVING UP FOR

ITEM DESCRIPTION	COST	WHERE TO GET IT	HAVE I GOT IT YET?

WAYS TO EARN MONEY

DATE	HOW TO EARN IT?	AMOUNT	HAVE I EARNED IT?

					TOTAL BALANCE: _____
DATE	NOTES	WITHDRAW	DEPOSIT	AMOUNT	TOTAL

SPECIFIC ITEMS I AM SAVING UP FOR

ITEM DESCRIPTION	COST	WHERE TO GET IT	HAVE I GOT IT YET?

WAYS TO EARN MONEY

DATE	HOW TO EARN IT?	AMOUNT	HAVE I EARNED IT?

				TOTAL BALANCE: _____	
DATE	NOTES	WITHDRAW	DEPOSIT	AMOUNT	TOTAL

SPECIFIC ITEMS I AM SAVING UP FOR			
ITEM DESCRIPTION	COST	WHERE TO GET IT	HAVE I GOT IT YET?

WAYS TO EARN MONEY			
DATE	HOW TO EARN IT?	AMOUNT	HAVE I EARNED IT?

			TOTAL BALANCE: _____		
DATE	NOTES	WITHDRAW	DEPOSIT	AMOUNT	TOTAL

SPECIFIC ITEMS I AM SAVING UP FOR			
ITEM DESCRIPTION	COST	WHERE TO GET IT	HAVE I GOT IT YET?

WAYS TO EARN MONEY			
DATE	HOW TO EARN IT?	AMOUNT	HAVE I EARNED IT?

				TOTAL BALANCE: _____	
DATE	NOTES	WITHDRAW	DEPOSIT	AMOUNT	TOTAL

TOTAL BALANCE: _____

DATE	NOTES	WITHDRAW	DEPOSIT	AMOUNT	TOTAL

		TOTAL BALANCE: _____			
DATE	NOTES	WITHDRAW	DEPOSIT	AMOUNT	TOTAL

TOTAL BALANCE: _____

DATE	NOTES	WITHDRAW	DEPOSIT	AMOUNT	TOTAL

| | | | TOTAL BALANCE: _____ |
DATE	NOTES	WITHDRAW	DEPOSIT	AMOUNT	TOTAL

TOTAL BALANCE: _____

DATE	NOTES	WITHDRAW	DEPOSIT	AMOUNT	TOTAL

TOTAL BALANCE: _____

DATE	NOTES	WITHDRAW	DEPOSIT	AMOUNT	TOTAL

				TOTAL BALANCE: _____
DATE	NOTES	WITHDRAW	DEPOSIT	AMOUNT	TOTAL
---	---	---	---	---	---

				TOTAL BALANCE: _____
DATE	NOTES	WITHDRAW	DEPOSIT	AMOUNT	TOTAL

				TOTAL BALANCE: _____
DATE	NOTES	WITHDRAW	DEPOSIT	AMOUNT	TOTAL

	TOTAL BALANCE: _____				
DATE	NOTES	WITHDRAW	DEPOSIT	AMOUNT	TOTAL

| | | | | TOTAL BALANCE: _____ | |
DATE	NOTES	WITHDRAW	DEPOSIT	AMOUNT	TOTAL

				TOTAL BALANCE: _____

DATE	NOTES	WITHDRAW	DEPOSIT	AMOUNT	TOTAL

			TOTAL BALANCE: _____		
DATE	NOTES	WITHDRAW	DEPOSIT	AMOUNT	TOTAL

TOTAL BALANCE: _____

DATE	NOTES	WITHDRAW	DEPOSIT	AMOUNT	TOTAL

DATE	NOTES	WITHDRAW	DEPOSIT	AMOUNT	TOTAL

TOTAL BALANCE: _____

TOTAL BALANCE: _____

DATE	NOTES	WITHDRAW	DEPOSIT	AMOUNT	TOTAL

| | | | | TOTAL BALANCE: _____ |
DATE	NOTES	WITHDRAW	DEPOSIT	AMOUNT	TOTAL

					TOTAL BALANCE: _____
DATE	NOTES	WITHDRAW	DEPOSIT	AMOUNT	TOTAL

DATE	NOTES	WITHDRAW	DEPOSIT	AMOUNT	TOTAL

TOTAL BALANCE: _____

				TOTAL BALANCE: _____	
DATE	NOTES	WITHDRAW	DEPOSIT	AMOUNT	TOTAL

				TOTAL BALANCE: _____

DATE	NOTES	WITHDRAW	DEPOSIT	AMOUNT	TOTAL

		TOTAL BALANCE: _____			
DATE	NOTES	WITHDRAW	DEPOSIT	AMOUNT	TOTAL

				TOTAL BALANCE: _____	
DATE	NOTES	WITHDRAW	DEPOSIT	AMOUNT	TOTAL

TOTAL BALANCE: _____

DATE	NOTES	WITHDRAW	DEPOSIT	AMOUNT	TOTAL

TOTAL BALANCE: _____

DATE	NOTES	WITHDRAW	DEPOSIT	AMOUNT	TOTAL

| | | TOTAL BALANCE: _____ | | | |
DATE	NOTES	WITHDRAW	DEPOSIT	AMOUNT	TOTAL

TOTAL BALANCE: _____

DATE	NOTES	WITHDRAW	DEPOSIT	AMOUNT	TOTAL

			TOTAL BALANCE: _____		
DATE	NOTES	WITHDRAW	DEPOSIT	AMOUNT	TOTAL

			TOTAL BALANCE: _____		
DATE	NOTES	WITHDRAW	DEPOSIT	AMOUNT	TOTAL

				TOTAL BALANCE: _____	
DATE	NOTES	WITHDRAW	DEPOSIT	AMOUNT	TOTAL

				TOTAL BALANCE: _____	
DATE	NOTES	WITHDRAW	DEPOSIT	AMOUNT	TOTAL

				TOTAL BALANCE: _____	
DATE	NOTES	WITHDRAW	DEPOSIT	AMOUNT	TOTAL

			TOTAL BALANCE: _____		
DATE	NOTES	WITHDRAW	DEPOSIT	AMOUNT	TOTAL

			TOTAL BALANCE: _____		
DATE	NOTES	WITHDRAW	DEPOSIT	AMOUNT	TOTAL

					TOTAL BALANCE: _____
DATE	NOTES	WITHDRAW	DEPOSIT	AMOUNT	TOTAL

			TOTAL BALANCE: _____		
DATE	NOTES	WITHDRAW	DEPOSIT	AMOUNT	TOTAL

TOTAL BALANCE: _____

DATE	NOTES	WITHDRAW	DEPOSIT	AMOUNT	TOTAL

		TOTAL BALANCE: _____			
DATE	NOTES	WITHDRAW	DEPOSIT	AMOUNT	TOTAL

				TOTAL BALANCE: _____	
DATE	NOTES	WITHDRAW	DEPOSIT	AMOUNT	TOTAL

				TOTAL BALANCE: _____	
DATE	NOTES	WITHDRAW	DEPOSIT	AMOUNT	TOTAL

				TOTAL BALANCE: _____	
DATE	NOTES	WITHDRAW	DEPOSIT	AMOUNT	TOTAL

			TOTAL BALANCE: _____		
DATE	NOTES	WITHDRAW	DEPOSIT	AMOUNT	TOTAL

				TOTAL BALANCE: _____	
DATE	NOTES	WITHDRAW	DEPOSIT	AMOUNT	TOTAL

					TOTAL BALANCE: _____
DATE	NOTES	WITHDRAW	DEPOSIT	AMOUNT	TOTAL

			TOTAL BALANCE: _____		
DATE	NOTES	WITHDRAW	DEPOSIT	AMOUNT	TOTAL

			TOTAL BALANCE: _____

DATE	NOTES	WITHDRAW	DEPOSIT	AMOUNT	TOTAL

| | | | | TOTAL BALANCE: _____ | |
DATE	NOTES	WITHDRAW	DEPOSIT	AMOUNT	TOTAL

		TOTAL BALANCE: _____			
DATE	NOTES	WITHDRAW	DEPOSIT	AMOUNT	TOTAL

			TOTAL BALANCE: _____		
DATE	NOTES	WITHDRAW	DEPOSIT	AMOUNT	TOTAL

TOTAL BALANCE: _____					
DATE	NOTES	WITHDRAW	DEPOSIT	AMOUNT	TOTAL

			TOTAL BALANCE: _____		
DATE	NOTES	WITHDRAW	DEPOSIT	AMOUNT	TOTAL

				TOTAL BALANCE: _____	
DATE	NOTES	WITHDRAW	DEPOSIT	AMOUNT	TOTAL

	TOTAL BALANCE: _____				
DATE	NOTES	WITHDRAW	DEPOSIT	AMOUNT	TOTAL

				TOTAL BALANCE: _____	
DATE	NOTES	WITHDRAW	DEPOSIT	AMOUNT	TOTAL

				TOTAL BALANCE: _____

DATE	NOTES	WITHDRAW	DEPOSIT	AMOUNT	TOTAL

				TOTAL BALANCE: _____	
DATE	NOTES	WITHDRAW	DEPOSIT	AMOUNT	TOTAL

				TOTAL BALANCE: _____	
DATE	NOTES	WITHDRAW	DEPOSIT	AMOUNT	TOTAL

				TOTAL BALANCE: _____	
DATE	NOTES	WITHDRAW	DEPOSIT	AMOUNT	TOTAL

				TOTAL BALANCE: _____

DATE	NOTES	WITHDRAW	DEPOSIT	AMOUNT	TOTAL

			TOTAL BALANCE: _____		
DATE	NOTES	WITHDRAW	DEPOSIT	AMOUNT	TOTAL

TOTAL BALANCE: _____

DATE	NOTES	WITHDRAW	DEPOSIT	AMOUNT	TOTAL

TOTAL BALANCE: _____

DATE	NOTES	WITHDRAW	DEPOSIT	AMOUNT	TOTAL

TOTAL BALANCE: _____

DATE	NOTES	WITHDRAW	DEPOSIT	AMOUNT	TOTAL

				TOTAL BALANCE: _____
DATE	NOTES	WITHDRAW	DEPOSIT	AMOUNT	TOTAL
---	---	---	---	---	---

TOTAL BALANCE: _____

DATE	NOTES	WITHDRAW	DEPOSIT	AMOUNT	TOTAL

				TOTAL BALANCE: _____
DATE	NOTES	WITHDRAW	DEPOSIT	AMOUNT	TOTAL
---	---	---	---	---	---

| | | | | TOTAL BALANCE: _____ | |
DATE	NOTES	WITHDRAW	DEPOSIT	AMOUNT	TOTAL

				TOTAL BALANCE: _____	
DATE	NOTES	WITHDRAW	DEPOSIT	AMOUNT	TOTAL

		TOTAL BALANCE: _____			
DATE	NOTES	WITHDRAW	DEPOSIT	AMOUNT	TOTAL

			TOTAL BALANCE: _____		
DATE	NOTES	WITHDRAW	DEPOSIT	AMOUNT	TOTAL

		TOTAL BALANCE: _____

DATE	NOTES	WITHDRAW	DEPOSIT	AMOUNT	TOTAL

			TOTAL BALANCE: _____		
DATE	NOTES	WITHDRAW	DEPOSIT	AMOUNT	TOTAL

TOTAL BALANCE: _____

DATE	NOTES	WITHDRAW	DEPOSIT	AMOUNT	TOTAL

			TOTAL BALANCE: _____		
DATE	NOTES	WITHDRAW	DEPOSIT	AMOUNT	TOTAL

					TOTAL BALANCE: _____
DATE	NOTES	WITHDRAW	DEPOSIT	AMOUNT	TOTAL

				TOTAL BALANCE: _____
DATE	NOTES	WITHDRAW	DEPOSIT	AMOUNT	TOTAL
---	---	---	---	---	---

DATE	NOTES	WITHDRAW	DEPOSIT	AMOUNT	TOTAL

TOTAL BALANCE: _____

DATE	NOTES	WITHDRAW	DEPOSIT	AMOUNT	TOTAL

TOTAL BALANCE: _____

				TOTAL BALANCE: _____	
DATE	NOTES	WITHDRAW	DEPOSIT	AMOUNT	TOTAL

				TOTAL BALANCE: _____	
DATE	NOTES	WITHDRAW	DEPOSIT	AMOUNT	TOTAL

| | | | TOTAL BALANCE: _____ | | |
DATE	NOTES	WITHDRAW	DEPOSIT	AMOUNT	TOTAL

Made in the USA
Coppell, TX
30 November 2019